D1410075

RHINOCEROSES

Katherine Walden

PowerKiDS press™

New York

For Sean Greene

Published in 2009 by The Rosen Publishing Group, Inc.
29 East 21st Street, New York, NY 10010

First Edition

Editor: Amelie von Zumbusch
Book Design: Erica Clendening
Layout Design: Julio Gil
Photo Researcher: Jessica Gerweck

Photo Credits: All images Shutterstock.com.

Library of Congress Cataloging-in-Publication Data

Walden, Katherine.
  Rhinoceroses / Katherine Walden.— 1st ed.
      p. cm. — (Safari animals)
  Includes index.
  ISBN-13: 978-1-4358-2687-8 (library binding) — ISBN 978-1-4358-3061-5 (pbk.)
ISBN 978-1-4358-3073-8 (6-pack)
  1. Rhinoceroses—Juvenile literature. I. Title.
  QL737.U63W34 2009
  599.66'8—dc22
                                        2008019534

Manufactured in the United States of America

CONTENTS

This big animal is a rhinoceros. Rhinoceroses are often called rhinos.

White rhinos are the world's biggest rhinos. They can weigh more than 6,000 pounds (2,722 kg).

Black rhinos are smaller than white rhinos. However, they still weigh as much as 3,000 pounds (1,361 kg).

9

Black rhinos and white rhinos both live on the **savannas** of Africa.

African rhinos have two **horns**. Rhinos use their horns to fight off enemies.

Rhinos eat plants. White rhinos eat mostly grass. Black rhinos like to eat leaves.

Rhinos eat in the morning or evening. They often sleep in the middle of the day, when it is very hot.

You can often see **oxpeckers** on a rhino. These birds eat bugs on the rhino's skin.

Baby rhinos are called **calves**. Rhino mothers take good care of their calves.

Young rhinos stay with their mothers until they are between two and four years old.

Words to Know

calf

horns

oxpecker

savanna

Index

O
oxpeckers,
  18

P
plants, 14

S
savannas,
  10
skin, 18

Web Sites

Due to the changing nature of Internet links, PowerKids Press has developed an online list of Web sites related to the subject of this book. This site is updated regularly. Please use this link to access the list:
www.powerkidslinks.com/safari/rhino/